❖

"A picture lives a life
like a living creature,
undergoing changes imposed
on us by our life from
day to day. This is natural
enough, as the picture
lives only through the man
who is looking at it."

Pablo Picasso

COME
LOOK WITH ME

Enjoying Art with Children

Gladys S. Blizzard

THOMASSON-GRANT
Charlottesville, Virginia

Published by Thomasson-Grant, Inc.
Designed by Lisa Lytton-Smith
Edited by Rebecca Beall Barns

98 97 96 95 94 93 92 91   5 4 3

Any inquiries should be directed to Thomasson-Grant, Inc.
One Morton Drive, Suite 500, Charlottesville, Virginia 22901
(804) 977-1780

Library of Congress
Cataloging-in-Publication Data
Blizzard, Gladys S.
    Come look with me: enjoying art with children / Gladys S.
Blizzard.
        p.   cm.
    Summary: Presents twelve color reproductions of paintings by
artists from Holbein to Picasso, with questions to stimulate discussion
and background information on each artist and painting.
    ISBN 0-934738-76-9
    1. Painting—Appreciation—Juvenile literature.   [1. Art
appreciation.]   I. Title.
ND1143.B53   1990
750'.1'1—dc20   90–19627
                                                        CIP
                                                        AC

THOMASSON-GRANT

Contents

Preface

The stimulus for COME LOOK WITH ME was my first grandchild, Julia Blair Sturm, and thus the book is dedicated to her. I wanted to share with her the pleasure of looking at art and of questioning it in ways that lead us to see and think beyond the obvious.

With the encouragement of family and friends, I selected these pictures and put together some questions for discussion. Professional guidance from Ruthe Battestin and Betty Cauthen along the way has helped turn an idea into reality.

I hope that grandparents, parents, teachers, and everyone who enjoys children will also enjoy sharing the ideas in this book.

How to use this book

Wherever I travel, I visit art museums and buy postcards of favorite paintings to send to my grandchild with a few questions that can be answered only after thoughtful looking. From an early age, my granddaughter has been interested in paintings of children. The topic has always seemed a natural one for discussion.

I find that while age, experience, and personal taste determine an individual's answers to questions about art, discussion with others brings depth, new insights, and the pleasure of shared experience. That is the purpose of this book.

COME LOOK WITH ME can be shared with one child or a small group of children. While the children look at the illustrations, an adult can read the background information silently, then read aloud or paraphrase, using it to stimulate and reinforce discussion. Ask the child to point to a part of the painting while he or she talks about it. In a group, find out if anyone has a different idea or opinion. It's probably best to discuss no more than two or three works of art at a time.

Most of the questions in this book are open-ended. There are no trick questions, no true or false answers. I hope they will spark lively discussions and get children more involved in what they see.

While this book is designed for home or school use, it is not intended to substitute for a trip to an art museum. Reproductions can't convey the size of the original painting or the texture of an artist's brush strokes. The book may, instead, help children learn how to look at paintings so that they will be able to see original works of art with greater understanding.

Children who learn how to look at art soon begin to enjoy discussions of what they see with family and friends. Eventually, children learn that we never finish looking at or learning from a work of art. It takes time to get to know a painting, just as it takes time to make friends.

PARVVLE PATRISSA, PATRIÆ VIRTVTIS ET HÆRES
ESTO, NIHIL MAIVS MAXIMVS ORBIS HABET.
GNATVM VIX POSSVNT COELVM ET NATVRA DEDISSE,
HVIVS QVEM PATRIS, VICTVS HONORET HONOS.
ÆQVATO TANTVM, TANTI TV FACTA PARENTIS,
VOTA HOMINVM, VIX QVO PROGREDIANTVR, HABENT
VINCITO, VICISTI. QVOT REGES PRISCVS ADORAT
ORBIS, NEC TE QVI VINCERE POSSIT, ERIT. Ricard Morysyn Car

HANS HOLBEIN THE YOUNGER. *Edward VI as a Child.* c. 1538. Oil on wood, 22 3/8″ x 17 3/8″.
National Gallery of Art, Washington, D.C., Andrew W. Mellon Collection.

How does this child compare to most one-year-olds you've seen?

What do you think the child is looking at?
What makes you think so?

The artist used a lot of different lines in this painting.
Find a straight line. Find a gently curving line. Find crossing
lines. Find a line with many curves.
Draw examples of the lines.

The Latin poem at the bottom of the portrait tells Edward VI to
be like his father. In what ways are you most like your parents?
In what ways are you different?

Hans Holbein's first art teacher was his father, who had the same
name. To avoid confusion between the father and son, they are identified
as Hans Holbein the Elder and Hans Holbein the Younger. When the
younger Holbein came to England from Switzerland, his pictures of people, called portraits, were very popular. Before the camera was invented,
people commissioned artists like Holbein to paint their portraits so that
they would be remembered. King Henry VIII asked the artist to become
his official court painter.

Holbein made this portrait of the King's son, Edward VI, when the
boy was little more than one year old. The prince's clothes make him look
very important. He wears a fancy hat decorated with an ostrich feather
and fine clothes made of red velvet and gold brocade. His left hand holds
a golden rattle, and his right hand is raised in a royal greeting.

FRANCISCO DE GOYA Y LUCIENTES. *Manuel Osorio Manrique de Zúñega.* c. 1787. Oil on canvas, 50″ x 40″.
The Metropolitan Museum of Art, New York, The Jules Bache Collection, 1949.

The boy is holding a string in his hands. Where does it go?
Why?

What do you think the boy is thinking about?

What do you think might happen to the bird?

Describe the boy's clothes. How do you think the clothes
would feel if you touched them?

Would you like to be dressed this way? Why?

When Goya was a young man, he painted scenes of everyday life in
Spain to decorate the king's royal palaces. Filled with light and bold
color, many of his paintings showed the happy side of life. In 1792, an ill-
ness left Goya deaf. Soon his art began to reflect a darker side of life,
especially the violence of war.

This portrait of Manuel Osorio, the son of a Spanish count, is one of
the first of Goya's commissioned portraits of children. The boy is dressed
in a scarlet suit trimmed in lace and satin, no doubt one of the best outfits
his parents could buy for him. Unaware of the danger to his pet bird, he
holds it on a string while the cats look on with big eyes. Goya printed the
boy's name at the bottom of the painting and signed his own name on the
card in the bird's beak.

SIR WILLIAM BEECHEY. *The Oddie Children.* 1789. Oil on canvas, 72" x 71 7/8".
The North Carolina Museum of Art, Raleigh, purchased with funds from the State of North Carolina.

Where are these children playing?

What is the weather? How did the artist show us that?

Do you think the boy's arrows are real? Why?

Compare the way these children are playing with the way you play.

How are your games different? How are your games the same?

One story of William Beechey's boyhood says that he enjoyed drawing so much that he found it difficult to do his schoolwork. He drew all over his lesson books instead. Raised by his uncle, who wanted him to be a lawyer, he was sometimes locked in the attic with nothing but his homework. One day he escaped and ran away to London, where he got a job painting carriages.

The stories of his boyhood adventures may or may not be true, but we do know that after attending art school, Beechey became well known as a portrait painter. There was a great demand for portraits in England then, and artists could make a good living this way. In 1789, he painted this picture of a brother and three sisters, the children of a prominent English lawyer.

JOSEPH WHITING STOCK. *Portrait of a Baby and Dog*. Date unknown. Oil on canvas, 36″ x 29″.
The Bennington Museum, Bennington, Vermont.

If you could touch this child's dress, how would it feel?

Can you think of two different words to describe the texture?

Why do you think the child is wearing a fancy dress?

Do you think this child feels happy or sad or friendly? Why?

When Joseph Whiting Stock was a child in the early 1800s, an accident paralyzed both of his legs. While he was confined to bed, he made toys for children to keep himself busy. His doctor also encouraged him to take art lessons so that he could draw and paint. Another doctor commissioned Stock to make drawings for him and became so interested in the boy that he designed and built a special wheelchair which made it possible for the artist to move around for the first time since his accident. The new chair enabled Stock to travel to towns in Massachussetts, Rhode Island, Connecticut, and New York to paint portraits and landscapes.

Many of the artist's portraits are of children in rooms decorated with rich colors and boldly patterned carpets. Usually the children have a cat or dog nearby and small toys like those the artist made when he was a child.

CHARLES BIRD KING. *Interior of a Ropewalk.* c. 1845. Oil on canvas, 39″ x 54 1/4″.
Bayly Art Museum at the University of Virginia, Charlottesville.

Count the people in the painting.
Count them again to make sure you didn't miss anyone.

Rope factories like this one were in very large buildings.
How has the artist shown us that the building is very long?

Why do you think the woman and children are here?

When Europeans settled in America, they needed rope for their work, especially on ships. There was once a ropewalk, or rope factory, like this one in most large towns.

Ropewalks were very large buildings where lengths of rope could be made and stretched out as long as two city blocks. One man fed hemp fibers to a big spinning wheel, while another man on the other side walked backward, placing the rope yarn on wooden pegs along the wall. Next, the yarns were twisted together to make coils of rope like those you see in the lower right corner of the painting.

Through the window, you can see the boat that brought hemp fiber to make the rope. In the ceiling, an opening reveals where the workers stored the fiber until it was needed.

The artist shows the size of this building through his skillful use of perspective. With light, shade, and line, he makes the building stretch out in front of the woman and two children who have come to see the factory.

JONATHAN EASTMAN JOHNSON. *The Old Stagecoach*. 1871. Oil on canvas, 36 1/4″ x 60 1/8″.
Milwaukee Art Museum, Layton Art Collection, Gift of Frederick Layton.

Do you think the children are having a good time?
What makes you think so?

If the painting suddenly came alive, what sounds would you
hear? Who or what would be making the sounds?
Can you make those sounds?

If you and your friends pretended you were traveling,
what would you play on? Draw a picture of it.

Jonathan Eastman Johnson's paintings show how country people dressed, worked, and played in America 100 years ago. The children in this painting are playing on an abandoned stagecoach, the kind of horse-drawn vehicle that once carried people from town to town. By 1871, when this scene was painted, railroads were already starting to replace stagecoaches for long trips.

The children pretend that the coach is moving, even though there are no wheels. Some of them make believe they are horses, passengers, and stagecoach drivers. The books on the ground and the warm afternoon light give us clues that the children have stopped here on the way home from school.

EDOUARD MANET. *Gare Saint-Lazare*. 1873. Oil on canvas, 36 3/4″ x 45 1/8″.
National Gallery of Art, Washington, D.C., Gift of Horace Havemeyer in memory of his mother, Louisine W. Havemeyer.

Why do you think the woman and girl are here?

What do you think the little girl is looking at so intently?

Can you find the color red in this painting? Where?

Describe the dog.

Why do you think there is a bunch of grapes in the lower right-hand corner of the painting?

The French word *gare* in the title of this painting means railroad station, and Gare Saint-Lazare is the name of a railroad station in Paris. When the French artist Edouard Manet painted this picture, train engines were run by the power of steam. The billowing whites and grays beyond the fence show us that a train is in the station. The little girl is watching the action, while the woman pauses from her quiet reading to look at us.

Manet painted more than 100 years ago in a style that continues to inspire artists to this day. He was one of the first artists to give as much attention to how a painting was painted as to the story it told. In his time, most people didn't like his bright colors and easy-to-see brush strokes. Manet's style gives this painting a feeling of motion and fills it with light.

WILLIAM-ADOLPHE BOUGUEREAU. *The Nut Gatherers.* 1882. Oil on canvas, 34 1/2" x 52 3/4".
©The Detroit Institute of Arts, Gift of Mrs. William E. Scripps.

Do you think these girls are sisters or friends? Why?

Do these girls look as if they have been playing?
What makes you think that?

What do you think these girls are thinking about?

This painting is made up of many details, such as a dimple in an elbow and folds in a skirt. How many details can you find?

William-Adolphe Bouguereau entered art school when he was 12 years old. The French artist painted texture and detail with remarkable clarity. He was considered one of the greatest painters of his time, though since then he has been criticized for making everything he painted look better than it really was. In this painting, for example, the girls have no dirt or stains on their bare feet, their hands, or their clothes, even though they have been collecting nuts in the dirt and grass.

JOHN G. BROWN. *A Tough Story.* 1886. Oil on canvas, 25" x 30".
The North Carolina Museum of Art, Raleigh, purchased with funds from the State of North Carolina.

How would you compare the clothes these boys are wearing to the clothes you wear?

Find the lightest brown and the darkest brown. Can you find a brown that has red in it? Can you find another brown that has yellow in it?

Do you think the artist liked these boys? How did he show that?

The boys seem to be interested in what their friend has to say. What do you think he's talking about?

John G. Brown was the most popular painter of American children in the 19th century. English by birth, he came to New York when he was a young man and took a job in a glass factory until he could begin his career as an artist. Some of his favorite subjects were the boys who worked and played in the city streets. They reminded him of his childhood in England.

In Brown's day, there were many popular stories about poor boys who were successful through resourcefulness and hard work. The boys in this painting are taking a break, resting on their shoeshine boxes while they listen to a story one of them has to tell.

PIERRE AUGUSTE RENOIR. *Two Young Girls at the Piano.* 1892. Oil on canvas, 44" x 34".
The Metropolitan Museum of Art, New York, Robert Lehman Collection, 1975.

Find something you could smell.

Find something you could hear.

Find something that would feel soft and silky.

Look carefully at one area of color and see if you can see other colors inside it. Can you name them?

Would you like to join these girls? Why?

When the French artist Pierre Auguste Renoir was 13 years old, he worked in a china factory, painting flowers on porcelain plates, cups, saucers, and vases. He later taught art and became well known for his "Impressionist" style of painting, in which he placed short brush strokes of color next to each other instead of blending the paint. This technique gives bright, shimmering color and a happy mood to his paintings. Renoir's favorite subjects were beautiful, rosy-cheeked women and children at play.

PABLO PICASSO. *Le Gourmet.* 1901. Oil on canvas, 36 1/2" x 26 7/8".
National Gallery of Art, Washington, D.C., Chester Dale Collection. Copyright © 1990 ARS N.Y./SPADEM.

What is the first thing you notice in this painting?

Why do you think this caught your eye before anything else?

What do you think is in the bowl?

Would you like to have this painting in your home? Why?

Pablo Picasso's life began in a dramatic way in a city along the southern coast of Spain. The midwife who delivered him thought he was born dead, but his uncle blew smoke in the baby's face and made him cry and breathe.

When the child was baptized, he was given ten names, but he signed his paintings with just one, Picasso, his mother's family name. Picasso could draw before he could talk. His father was a museum curator and an artist, and from the start, he encouraged his son's creativity.

After traveling to see more of the world, Picasso decided to live and work in France. He painted *Le Gourmet* (which in the French language means someone who knows a lot about food) when he was only 19 years old. This was a time in his life when he felt very sad and saw much sadness around him. He showed this in the cool blue color which dominated his paintings. The heavy, flowing lines in the girl's hair, in her dress, and in the big cloth napkin around her neck keep our eyes moving over the painting.

PABLO PICASSO. *Maya with a Doll.* 1938. Oil on canvas, 28 3/4″ x 23 5/8″.
Private Collection. Copyright © 1990 ARS N.Y./SPADEM.

Maya with a Doll was painted by the same artist as *Le Gourmet*. Would you know that by looking at the paintings? Which do you like better? Why?

How many circles can you find? How many half circles can you find? How many triangles can you find? How many squares can you find? How many rectangles can you find?

This imaginative style of painting presents subjects from more than one view. Look carefully at someone near you. Look straight in the person's face. Look at the profile, or the side of the person's face. Look at the face of the child in the painting. Find the part of her face that is the profile.

Can you sit with your legs and feet in the same position as this child? How are your legs and feet different?

After Picasso painted *Le Gourmet*, he began experimenting with a style of painting that reduces images to geometric shapes, sharp edges, and angles. In this style, called Cubism, noses sometimes look like cones and eyes like triangles. By drawing the human face this way, Picasso was able to show us views from the front and side at the same time. In some of his paintings, like this one of his daughter, people look like puzzles that haven't been put back together the right way.

Picasso is probably the most famous artist of the 20th century. No matter how well he did something, he always challenged himself to try something new. His way of seeing has changed ideas about beauty and opened art to new ways of thinking.

Go back and look at all the paintings again.

Choose one as a favorite for today.

Open the book so that it will stand up. Place it on a table or shelf so you can look at the painting as you pass by.

Look at the paintings another day, and you'll be surprised at how much more you'll see.

Keep looking!